21 Ways to Close Sales Now

Eric Lofholm

Eric Lofholm International, Inc.
3031 Stanford Ranch Road, Suite 2-132, Rocklin, CA 95765
888.81.SALES
www.ericlofholm.com

Book Cover by BJ Design & Pear Creations

Acknowledgments

I would like to thank the following people for helping me create this book. Everyone mentioned is a mentor or inspiration to me in some way.

Dr. Donald Moine has had a tremendous impact on my life in so many ways.

Dante Perano, Tony Martinez, Jonathan Dune, Tony Robbins and Ted Thomas have all invested time in training me about business and life.

Jay Abraham, Napoleon Hill and Mark Victor Hansen have influenced me through their books.

My mom introduced me to personal development. She also edited this book. Thank you, Mom, for all of your support and encouragement through the years.

My dad has inspired me to be a business owner and a professional speaker.

My wife of 14 years, Jarris, is the mother of our two beautiful children, Brandon and Sarah, and has supported me in countless ways.

Warren Jamison helped me turn my ideas into words for this book.

In appreciation,
Eric

Introduction

Professional selling is one of the most interesting professions in the world, unique because it offers all of us the opportunity to earn what we're worth. Because of this fact, becoming good at sales is vital since our skill sets directly affect our income.

Napoleon Hill, author of *Think and Grow Rich,* said, "One good idea is all one needs to achieve great success." This idea is true in sales when restated in this way, "One good idea is all one needs to greatly increase sales results."

For example, a few years ago I averaged 2 referrals per sales appointment. Then I learned a way to increase my referrals-per-meeting average. I implemented this single idea, and my referrals-per-meeting average went up to 10, a 500 percent increase from just one idea!

In one appointment I got a whopping 67 referrals. I estimate that I have earned more than $100,000 in commissions from the extra referrals I got using that one idea.

Right now in this moment, you are just one good idea away from significantly increasing your income. That's what this book is for: to generate sales ideas that will help you create the results you want.

The first idea I'll share with you is a way of thinking. Every day I use the thought process I am going to teach you. Once you learn this thought process, you will have it for the rest of your selling career. The thought process is called the baseline strategy. Your sales baseline is a combination of all of your selling skills and selling actions right now. It is your goal setting, your time management skill, your ability to handle objections, your sales presentation skill and your phone skill. Everything you bring to the table as a sales professional right now is your baseline.

The baseline strategy is to keep doing what you are doing to create results as a sales professional and add one new idea or one new strategy. For example, let's say that at the end of your sales presentation, you are not currently asking for referrals. If you added that to your presentation, you would continue to create the results you already are achieving plus whatever referrals you get.

In *21 Ways to Close More Sales Now,* you will be introduced to 21 different ideas to add to your baseline. You may already be using some of the strategies in this book. Let's say you are already using 12 of the 21 ideas in this book. Focus on the 9 strategies you aren't doing. You are just one good idea away from starting to create the results you desire.

To get the most out of this book, buy a journal. Have it with you while you read. This will allow you to capture the good ideas. Write down how you will use the ideas in your selling.

My vision is to have more than a million sales professionals, network marketers, sales managers and executives read *21 Ways to Close More Sales Now.* I can only achieve this vision with your help. The best advertising is word of mouth. As you get value from this book, encourage others to go to www.ericlofholm.com and pick up a copy for themselves. A great way to let others know is to email my website, www.ericlofholm.com, to your sales friends and encourage them to get this book. Also, it's a great idea to tell your sales team or network marketing team about *21 Ways to Close More Sales Now* at your next meeting.

The second edition of *21 Ways to Close More Sales Now* will include testimonials of salespeople just like you who have taken the ideas and strategies in this book and translated them into more sales. When you implement these ideas and close more sales, please email your successes to me, eric@ericlofholm.com. I will put the best stories in the next edition.

The Structure of the Book

Each of the 21 ways to close more sales consists of a section which includes a question, a rating, a success tip and an exercise.

The Power of Questions

Your brain works like a computer. If you ask yourself a question, your brain will answer it. For example, ask yourself, "What is my favorite beverage when I wake up in the morning?" You most likely got an answer such as coffee, orange juice, milk or tea. The key point is that your brain answered the question. I have enclosed a sales question in each chapter to stimulate thinking on your part.

The Benefit of Rating Yourself

The first step toward improving is to take an inventory of where you are now and decide where you want to go. The difference between where you are and where you want to go is the gap. Once you have established where you are, where you want to go and the gap, you can create an action plan to achieve your goals. Each section of this book has a rating question to assist you in identifying where you are at that moment.

One Idea – All You Need to Achieve Success

Each section contains a success tip, an especially useful idea.

Action – The Key Ingredient of Success

Each section contains an exercise. One measure of your determination to increase your success and income is how thoroughly you complete the exercises. Each exercise is designed to help you implement the idea. I have met many salespeople who read a lot of books and learn many great ideas, but they have not acted on the knowledge learned. This book is not entertainment; its purpose is to provide specific strategies to increase your sales results and then to inspire you to action.

Successfully yours,
Eric

Contents

1. Create a Testimonial Book

I have closed hundreds of sales with the help of my testimonial book. It works because one of the most powerful ways to influence someone is with a testimonial from a third party. This is why major advertisers pay millions of dollars to celebrities and athletes to endorse their products and services. However, you don't have to pay anyone to endorse you. Simply go to your satisfied clients and ask them for a written endorsement. Once you have the letters, display them nicely in plastic pages in a binder. You can purchase the plastic pages at your local office supply store.

Ralph Roberts is America's number one real estate salesperson. Ralph calls his book his presentation folder. Here is what Ralph has to say about his presentation folder in his book *52 Weeks of Sales Success:*

> My presentation folder is a large-format, zippered leather binder in which I have mounted photos of my family, a picture of my 'U WIN' license plate, copies of awards or honors that I've received, even photos of my Corvette and of my wife and me in our hot tub at home. When I meet new clients, I tell them my personal story, flipping through the pages of my folder to illustrate…. Today I'm training all my assistants to develop their own presentation folders.

I taught Bill Mayer the strategy of creating a testimonial book. Bill implemented this one idea. He shared with me that he closed a sale with the help of his book. He told me he didn't believe he would have closed the sale without his book. His commission was more than $20,000 on this sale alone!

Here are hints for creating a book that will boost your sales:
- Put a cover on the testimonial book, and call it your *Raving Fans Book*.
- Put pictures in your book showing that you are successful.
- Purchase a quality binder. The nicer the binder, the more impressed your prospect will be.

Here are some ways you can use your testimonial book:
- Incorporate the book into your sales presentation.
- Whenever you interview for a job, bring the book with you. You will almost certainly get the job.
- Let clients look at the book while you complete paperwork.

Question

What are some ways I could use a testimonial book to increase my sales?

Rating

On a scale of 1 to 10, how effectively do I use third-party endorsements in my sales presentations?

Success Tip

An easy way to get a written endorsement is to provide your clients with a fill-in-the-blanks customer service survey. People are conditioned to filling out forms. After you complete the sale, ask your client to complete the fill-in-the-blank customer service survey. Select the best ones, and put them in your book.

Exercise

In the next 7 days, go to an office supply store, such as Staples, and purchase a binder and 25 clear plastic pages. The binder will become your testimonial book. The plastic pages will allow you to display your testimonials. Ω

2. Go Back to Existing Customers

One of the first steps in any sales process is to create rapport with the customer. It has often been said that people do business with people they like and trust. It is very difficult to make a sale to someone who doesn't trust you. Because of this fact, one of the best opportunities for most salespeople is to go back to their existing customers and make another offer to them. Common strategies to contact your customers are direct mail, telemarketing and email. I make hundreds of sales each year going back to my existing customers. If you have heard this idea before, ask yourself, "How effectively am I contacting my existing customers for repeat sales?"

Question

What would it mean to me if I consistently contacted my existing customers for additional sales?

Rating

On a scale of 1 to 10, how effective am I at going back to my existing customers for additional sales?

Success Tip

When people hear an idea or strategy they're already familiar with, they often immediately dismiss the idea by saying, "I already know that." Don't allow yourself to make this critical mistake. When you read or hear an idea you have heard before, ask yourself this question: How effectively am I in actually using this idea in my business now?

Exercise

Identify your top 10 customers. Contact them in the next 7 days. Ask them for additional business and referrals. Ω

3. Invigorate Your Selling Habits

The quality of their habits separates super sales professionals from average sales professionals. As much as 90% of our behavior is determined by our habits.

If you were to change a couple of bad sales habits into good sales habits, you could possibly double your sales. For example, you may have the habit of not asking for referrals on sales calls. If you develop the habit of asking for referrals, the number of referrals you generate will skyrocket. This is a very simple idea. Do not be fooled by its simplicity. For most sales professionals, changing just a couple of bad habits will result in thousands of dollars in increased income.

Questions

What are my best selling habits?
What are my worst selling habits?

Rating

On a scale of 1 to 10, how do I rate my good selling habits?

Success Tip

Talk to successful sales professionals, and ask them what their best selling habits are.

Exercises

Make a list of your 5 worst selling habits.
Make a list of your 5 best selling habits. Ω

4. Hire an Assistant

One of the most effective ways to leverage your time is to hire assistants. In most cases you can hire an assistant for $8 to $25 per hour. I have 2 assistants: an administrative assistant and a telemarketing assistant. Another type of assistant is a consultant. Consultants are hired on an as-needed basis. Typically they charge from $25 to $300 per hour. The benefit consultants provide is highly specialized help, but you don't have to put them on the payroll. I use consultants to do my website work and my accounting. It would not be cost effective for me to hire a web person or an accountant full time, so I hire consultants.

"How do I know when I'm ready to hire an assistant?" you might be asking yourself.

This is a very common question that has a simple answer. Hiring an assistant is a financial decision. Determine how many hours you would have your assistant work. Decide how much you are going to pay your assistant. Let's say you were going to hire an assistant to work 20 hours per week at $10 per hour – $200 per week. Ask yourself, "If I had an assistant right now working 20 hours per week, could I increase my income more than $200 per week?" If the answer is yes, then you should strongly consider hiring an assistant.

A question to think about: What if you hired an assistant at a cost of $1,000 per month and as a result you increased your income by $4,000 per month? Perhaps you could take the extra $3,000 and invest it into advertising and boost your business again.

Question

If you don't have an assistant: If I had an assistant right now, what would it allow me to do?

If you have an assistant: Do I need a second assistant?

Rating (if you have an assistant)

On a scale of 1 to 10, how effectively do I use my assistant(s)?

Success Tip

Do what you do best, and hire others to do the rest.
A great way to increase your sales is to hire others to help your sales effort.

Exercise

Write in your journal how you would use an assistant if you were to hire one.

If you already have one assistant, write down how you would use a second assistant. Ω

5. Model a Top Producer

Success leaves clues. In many cases, becoming a top producer can be achieved by modeling other top producers. By modeling, I mean emulating their actions and adapting their methods to your own personality.

Excellence and achievement have a structure. When you model others, focus on their beliefs and their strategies. You can model others by reading their books, listening to their tapes, attending their seminars or taking them out to lunch.

People often ask me to share with them techniques on how they can become better closers. The most powerful strategy I have ever learned to improve closing is to go on live sales calls with master closers. Watch everything they do.

Observe

• How they dress.
• How they create rapport.
• How they ask for the order.
• What time they show up for the sales call.
• How they handle objections.
• How they up sell.
• The stories they tell in the sales presentation.

Question

What successful person in my industry can I model?

Rating

On a scale of 1 to 10, how effectively do I model others?

Success Tip

Take successful salespeople out to lunch. Ask them questions to identify the beliefs and strategies that make them successful.

Exercise

Make of list of the top 5 salespeople you know. Call each of them in the next week, and ask if you can go with them on a live sales call. Ω

6. Write Down Your Goals

Strategy 6 is deceptively simple. I often ask the audience at my sales mastery seminars if they believe goal setting is important in selling. They always answer yes. I then ask them to raise their hand if they have written sales goals with a written action plan for each goal. Very few hands go up. Almost everyone agrees that goal setting is important, yet few people do it. Do you have written sales goals with a written action plan for each goal?

Ben Feldman was at one time the greatest insurance salesperson in the world. There were many things that made Ben successful. Goal setting was one of them. Ben's first sales goal was to earn $35 per week. He achieved that goal. His next sales goal was to earn $45 per week. He achieved that goal. He continued to set higher and higher goals until he became the most successful insurance salesperson in the world. Ben averaged $25,000,000 in sales over nearly 40 years!

Questions

What is my major life goal?

What are my 3 most important goals right now?

Rating

On a scale of 1 to 10, how do I rate myself in goal setting?

Two Success Tips

Have one place to record your goals, like a writing journal or a computer file. Make it easy to find your goals when you want to work on them.

Clearly define what you want. The most successful people in the world clearly define their goals. It's not enough to say, "I want to make more money." Clearly define how much more you would like to make and precisely how you'll do it.

Exercise

Spend 30 minutes today writing down your sales goals for the year, the month and the week. Ω

7. Create a Written Plan for Each Selling Day

Imagine 2 salespeople, Arnie and Ben, who have similar abilities. Arnie has a written plan for the day; Ben does not. Assuming all other factors are equal, will Arnie or Ben produce the best results? Of course, Arnie will.

Do you consistently plan your sales day in writing? What would it mean to your sales production if you did? Here is a simple, yet powerful, strategy for planning your day.

There are 1,440 minutes in every 24-hour day. Each 14 minutes is 1 percent of the day. Spend 14 minutes planning each day. Create a list of everything you need to accomplish. Once you have created the list, identify the 2 most important outcomes on the list. Put an asterisk next to the 2 most important outcomes.

Question

What would it mean to me if I consistently planned my day?

Rating

On a scale of 1 to 10, how do I rate at planning my day?

Success Tip

Write your plan in a day planner or Palm Pilot each day.

Exercise

For the next week spend 14 minutes each day planning. Identify your top 2 outcomes each day. Ω

8. Learn from Books, Audiotapes & Seminars

One of the fastest ways to get a raise in the business world is to be one of the professional salespeople who are improving their skills. For example, by improving your closing skills, you will make more money. Once you learn how to be an effective closer, you will have those skills for the rest of your life. A great way to improve your skills is to read books, listen to audiotapes and attend seminars.

Question

What sales book will I read next?

Rating

On a scale of 1 to 10, how do I rate at studying sales books and tapes?

Success Tip

If you do a lot of driving, turn your car into a university on wheels by using your drive time to listen to sales and success audiotapes.

Exercise

Ask your manager what training materials the company provides. Also find out about your company's policy on paying for you to go to sales-increasing seminars. Ω

9. Use Technology

Advances in technology have improved the sales results of thousands of salespeople all over the world. I use technology to plan my day (Palm Pilot), set goals (goal setting software), generate leads (website), keep in touch with clients (email) and countless other uses.

Questions

How can I use technology to increase my sales results?

What are some ways I can use technology more effectively?

Rating

On a scale of 1 to 10, how do I rate in using technology as a selling tool?

Success Tip

Some salespeople are experts at using technology to increase sales. Identify these individuals and interview them to learn their secrets.

Exercise

Here are several different technology resources: software, desktop computer, laptop computer, Palm Pilot, database (ACT, Goldmine, Outlook), Internet, website, email. List 10 ways you can use these technology resources to increase your sales. Ω

10. Get More Referrals

For many salespeople, getting more referrals provides a huge opportunity to increase results. In general, salespeople are either really good at getting referrals or really bad. The ones who are really bad tend to be bad because they don't have a systematic way to get referrals.

One of the best ways to improve results in the area of referrals is to have a referral system. A great way to develop a referral system is to find out what others in your industry are doing and model them.

The example that I gave in the beginning of the book, in which I increased my referrals from 2 referrals per meeting to 10 referrals per meeting, was learned by modeling a top producer in my industry.

Who is effective at getting referrals in your industry? If you don't already know, find out. How? Ask everybody and anybody who might know. Find out what they do to get referrals.

One of the most powerful ideas for getting referrals is to have a referral outcome for your sales calls. Many of my coaching clients want me to help them improve in the area of referrals. First, I always ask them, "When you go on a sales call, what is your outcome?" The most common answer is, "My outcome is to make a sale." I then ask them if they have any other outcomes. They almost always say, "No."

This is why they are not getting referrals. You get what you focus on. If you have an outcome to get 3 referrals on your sales call, chances are you will. From now on, define your referral outcome for each sales call. If you haven't been getting any referrals at all, set your original goal at getting 1 per sales call. Raise your goal each time you establish a new high in your average number of referrals per call.

Question

What are my best referral opportunities right now?

Rating

On a scale of 1 to 10, how do I rate at getting referrals?

Success Tip

Develop a referral script. Here is one of my scripts. I have received more than 1,000 referrals using this script.

> As you probably know, I work with referrals. A good referral for me is a sales manager or network marketing leader who has a team of 6 or more salespeople in Southern California. When you think of a good referral, think of where you have worked in the past, other offices that your company has, where your clients work. Of everyone you know, who would be the 3 best referrals for you?

Exercise

For the next week ask for referrals on every sales call. Ω

11. Achieve Mastery

I have trained thousands of salespeople. Most salespeople's selling skill sets are strong enough to get by. They can close sales effectively enough to produce sales results. They are effective enough on the phone to produce sales results. In general, they are effective enough in the various areas of selling to produce results, yet they haven't mastered a single area.

The strategy of mastery is to look at the selling skills you use on a daily basis. Identify the one selling skill that, if mastered, would produce the greatest result. Once you have identified that skill, create a written action plan to master it.

One of my favorite stories of mastery is about Tiger Woods, the golfer. Tiger won $60,000,000 in prize money and endorsements in his first year in golf competition. In Tiger's second year he won the Masters by the largest margin of victory in the history of the tournament.

After winning the Masters, Tiger watched footage of the tournament with his golf coach. Together they decided that he had not yet mastered his swing. Tiger made the decision with the help of his coach to reinvent his golf swing from scratch. He wanted to master his swing. Tiger's results went down as he began to reinvent his swing. He only won 1 tournament over the next 18 months. He continued to work toward mastery.

One day it all came together. Tiger went on to win 10 of his next 14 tournaments. He won 7 straight tournaments in one stretch. He then went on to become the first golfer in history to win the 4 majors in a row. I believe he accomplished this because of his commitment to mastery.

Question

What is the one selling skill that, if mastered, would produce the biggest result?

Rating

Take your answer from the mastery question above and apply that answer to the rating question.

On a scale of 1 to 10, how do I rate myself in _____ ? For example, if you said prospecting was the skill that, if mastered, would produce the biggest result, then ask yourself, "On a scale of 1 to 10, how do I rate myself in prospecting?"

Success Tip

Practice is one of the most important actions you can take when it comes to mastering anything.

Exercise

Identify the one area of your business that, if mastered, would produce the greatest result. Ω

12. Discover Where the Money Is

Here's one of the most powerful sales ideas on the planet: Where is the money? The strategy is only 16 words long. These 16 words, when acted upon, have the ability to double your sales or even more.

The strategy is simple and profound at the same time. Implementing the idea could catapult you into your company's top producer rank within 90 days. Implementing the idea could change the way you approach your sales day, every day, for the rest of your selling career.

Here are the magical 16 words: **Identify the sales activities that will produce the greatest sales results, and focus on those activities.**

Question

What are the activities that will produce the greatest sales results?

Rating

On a scale of 1 to 10, how do I rate at focusing on the activities that will produce the greatest sales results?

Success Tip

Ask others in your industry what they feel are the sales activities that will produce the greatest sales results. You can learn from their answers.

Exercise

Make a list of activities that will produce the greatest sales results in your business. Ω

13. Use the Law of Averages

Sales is a numbers-driven industry. Your sales results can be broken down into ratios of results. If you make 10,000 calls and you set 500 appointments, then your close ratio on appointments is 1:20; you set 1 appointment every 20 calls.

Step 1 is to know the ratios in your business.

Step 2 is to run the numbers. Here is an example of running the numbers: suppose your goal is to set 5 meetings this week and you close 1 of 20 calls. This means you need to make 100 calls to set 5 appointments. Your job then would be to make sure that you make 100 calls this week.

Prior to the beginning of each month, I identify my sales goals for the upcoming month. Based on my goals and based on the numbers in my industry, I create an action plan to achieve my goals. For example, in my company we average $500 in revenue per sales call. If our goal is $30,000 in revenue from these sales calls, then we need to run 60 appointments. If I didn't know that we average $500 per sales call, I wouldn't know how many sales calls we would need to make to hit our goal.

If you don't know the numbers in your industry, it could be greatly affecting your overall results.

Question

What are the numbers in my business? If you don't know the answer, find someone who does.

Rating

On a scale of 1 to 10, how do I rate at knowing the numbers (sales ratios) in my business? On a scale of 1 to 10, how do I rate at running the numbers in my business?

Success Tip

Begin each month with written sales goals. Use your understanding of the law of averages to help you create a written plan to achieve your sales goals. Say you sell cars, and your goal is to sell 15 cars this month. If you sell 1 car out of every 3 test drives that you conduct, then you need to go on 45 test drives for the month.

Exercise

Meet with your manager, and ask what he or she believes the numbers are in your industry. Ω

14. Practice Your Close

Closing the sale is an important part of selling because this is how we get paid. Most of us get a percentage of the revenue we generate by closing. Professional actors practice their lines. Professional salespeople practice their closes. If you don't have your close written down, I urge you to commit it to paper, better yet, to your computer screen, so that you can polish it. It's easier to practice if you have your close written. You can practice your close by yourself or role play with a co-worker.

Question
What would it mean to me if I mastered my close?

Rating
On a scale of 1 to 10, how do I rate in closing?

Success Tip
Learn the close so well that you can recite it from memory.

Exercise
Go on a live sales call with a master closer in the next 30 days. Ω

15. Master Objections

Typically, some of between 7 and 12 common objections will come up during any given sales presentation. Many sales presentations get stymied when this happens. Since getting objections is inevitable in selling, you must be prepared to overcome them.

Because there are usually only a dozen of these common objections, it's easy to prepare effective responses to them. The best way to start mastering objections is to write down the common objections in your business. Next, write 3 to 5 responses you could use in different situations. Then practice those responses.

Question
What objection gives me the most difficulty?

Rating
On a scale of 1 to 10, how do I rate at handling objections?

Success Tip
Create an audiocassette that has the common objections and your responses on it. Listen to the tape while you drive.

Exercise
Make a list of the common objections in your industry. Develop 3 or more responses per objection. Keep a book of the most powerful responses to each objection. Ω

16. Define Your Outcomes Before Each Sales Call

You get what you focus on. Because I have found that statement to be true, I define my outcomes before each sales call. By outcomes, I mean the results I want from my sales call. Here are some examples of outcomes you might have:

- Make a sale.
- Get a referral.
- Recruit the prospect into your organization (multi-level marketing presentation).
- Get a purchase order signed.
- Sell a specific volume or quantity.

Question

What are my outcomes for this sales call?

Rating

On a scale of 1 to 10, how do I rate at defining my outcomes prior to my sales calls?

Success Tip

Look for desirable outcomes to define for each sales call.

Exercise

Set a goal to define your outcomes on every sales call that you make for the rest of your life. Ω

17. Act As If
You Will Achieve Your Sales Goals

The human mind has amazing power. One way to harness this astounding power is to act as if your goals will be realized.

Your mind operates in 3 compartments: the past, the present and the future. You have the ability to imagine achieving your goals in the future Let's say your goal is to earn $100,000 in the next 12 months. If you knew you were going to do that, what actions would you take to achieve your goal? Begin now to take the actions consistent with earning $100,000 in the next 12 months.

Jim Carrey, the comedian, used to act as if he were one of the wealthiest people in the world. Years ago, he lived in a van, but now he is one of the world's wealthiest people. One success technique that he used to achieve these results was the "as if" principle.

When Jim Carrey was starting his career in comedy, he wrote himself a check for $10,000,000. On the pay-to-the-order-of line, he wrote his name. On the memo line of the check he wrote, "for action services rendered." He dated the check November 24, 1995. For a few years, Jim carried the check in his wallet everywhere he went. Jim began to act "as if" he were going to cash the check on that date.

He began to take the actions of a comedian who would command a $10,000,000 payday. He went to every audition he could. He spent hours every day looking at himself in the mirror, teaching himself how to make funny expressions. For several years, he acted "as if" he were going to cash that check. Within 30 days of the due date, he did cash the check for exactly $10,000,000.

Here is the formula:

1. Choose a goal.
2. Ask yourself, "If I knew I were going to achieve (your goal) by (achievement date), what actions would I take?
3. Write down the action steps.
4. Begin to act as if you were going to accomplish your goal.

Question

What goal can I select today to pursue by acting as if I were going to accomplish it?

Success Tip

Use the "as if" principle to help you in all areas of goal setting, not just sales.

Exercise

Make a list of the actions a salesperson would need to take in order to become the top producer in your industry. Ω

18. Sell the Benefits

I often ask my audience in my sales mastery seminars, "In a hardware store, what do drill salesmen sell?" The audience will usually say, "They sell drills." Then I tell the audience that drill salesmen don't sell drills, they sell the holes the drills will make. People want benefits.

Because I am a sales trainer, I will often sit through sales presentations to see how others try to influence me. In many of those presentations, the salesperson has made the mistake of either not selling the benefits of the product or service, or has tried to sell me the benefits that interested him.

This raises an interesting question. How do you know what benefits the customer is interested in? The answer is, first, you must ask them, and second, you must listen to the answer. That is the reason we have 2 ears and only 1 mouth. Many salespeople could double their sales by listening better, by learning how to find out what benefits interest a given customer and then by selling him or her on those benefits.

There are 2 types of benefits, direct and indirect. Direct benefits are measurable and tangible. When you purchase a car, one direct benefit could be a 10-disc CD changer. An indirect benefit is one that you receive as a result of having the car. You might feel more confident in your new convertible, for example.

Which is more important, the direct or indirect benefit? You're right; the more important benefit is the one that customers feel is more important to them.

Rating

On a scale of 1 to 10, how do I rate at selling the benefits?

Question

What are the most powerful benefits my product or service offers?

Success Tip

Ask other salespeople on your team what they feel are the benefits that your product or service offers.

Exercise

Write down as many direct benefits and indirect benefits your product or service offers. This is a great exercise to do with your sales or network marketing team. Ω

19. Do What You Know

Strategy 19 is the most powerful idea I have presented so far. Students of sales, like you, often know things they could be doing that would make them a lot of money if they used them.

"What is one idea I can implement today that will immediately increase my sales?" Salespeople at my seminars often ask.

"Do what you know," I answer.

Question

How can I get better at doing what I know with my clients?

Rating

On a scale of 1 to 10, how do I rate at doing what I know with customers?

Success Tip

Every 90 days ask yourself, "What do I know?"

Exercise

Make a list of all of the actions you know you should be taking to produce better sales results. Ω

20. Use a Script

Sales scripts are one of the most misunderstood areas of selling. In my sales mastery seminars, I often ask how many people use scripts. In most cases it is fewer than half.

The number one reason salespeople give for not wanting to use scripts is they don't want to sound canned or scripted. If I believed that I sounded canned when I used a script, I wouldn't use one either. Here is the truth about scripts: The most successful sales professionals in the world use scripts, but you don't know it. They are so good at it that they become the script.

The largest benefit of using a script is that it allows you to produce consistent results. Think about a script the way a great actor or actress does: become the script. They are so good at it that many people who meet them in real life expect the actor/actress to be like they are in the movie or TV role they play.

What would happen to your sales if you became so good at your scripts that if they gave an Oscar in selling, you would be the one to receive it?

Think about this: Radio and TV ads are scripted so that they will produce consistent results. People who place radio and TV ads want to maximize their advertising investment, so they use the most powerful words possible.

Question

What scripts do I need?

Rating

On a scale of 1 to 10, how do I rate at effectively using sales scripts?

Success Tip

Find the best script writer on your sales team. Ask him or her to help you create powerful scripts.

Exercise

Make a list of all of the scripts you need in your business. Prioritize the list. Create the scripts, one by one. Ω

21. Take Action

Action is the most powerful idea in this entire book. Ideas by themselves are worthless; good ideas put into action are priceless. They will help you create the life of your dreams. It is great to learn new ideas, but learning is not enough. You must take consistent action. You have learned 21 ways to close more sales now. Next, do the exercise below.

Question

What is the single area of selling that, if I took more action, I would see an increase in my sales results?

Rating

On a scale of 1 to 10, how do I rate at taking consistent action in my selling career?

Success Tip

It's amazing how long it takes to accomplish a task you're not working on.

Exercise

Look at the 21 ways to close more sales now.

1.   Create a Testimonial Book

2.   Go Back to Existing Customers

3.   Invigorate Your Selling Habits

4.   Hire an Assistant

5.   Model a Top Producer

6.   Write Down Your Goals

7.   Create a Written Plan for Each Selling Day

8.   Learn from Books, Audiotapes & Seminars

9. Use Technology

10. Get More Referrals

11. Achieve Mastery

12. Discover Where the Money Is

13. Use the Law of Averages

14. Practice Your Close

15. Master Objections

16. Define Your Outcomes Before Each Sales Call

17. Act As If You Will Achieve Your Sales Goals

18. Sell the Benefits

19. Do What You Know

20. Use a Script

21. Take Action

Pick one of the ways and take action. Once you have implemented the idea, come back to the list and select another idea and take action. Ω

A Final Note from The Author

Now that you have read *21 Ways to Close More Sales Now*, you are ready to begin reaping the rewards of your new knowledge. The book is designed to teach you the baseline strategy, to teach you 21 ways to improve your baseline and to be a sales idea generator. Use this book to help you generate great sales ideas for the rest of your selling career.

As I shared with you in the beginning of the book, my vision is for a million salespeople, sales managers, network marketers and executives to read *21 Ways to Close More Sales Now*. Help me achieve this goal while helping your friends and co-workers in sales by sharing with them how they can get their own copy of the book, which is available online at www.ericlofholm.com.

Also remember to share your success stories with me so that I can include your great news in the next edition, as well as on my website.

Free Sales Audio

7 Secrets to Sales Greatness
by Eric Lofholm

To receive this free sales audio, go to:

www.7secretstosalesgreatness.com

Enter your email address, and you will
immediately be emailed the audio download.

This audio is free to you and everyone in your network.
Tell everyone you know in sales about this free audio.
www.7secretstosalesgreatness.com

Free Sales Training Conference Call

Join Eric Lofholm
on his next free sales training conference call,
How to Become a Sales Superstar

To register for the call, go to:
www.ericlofholm.com/conference-call.php

On this call you will learn:

- The most common mistakes salespeople make and how to avoid them.
- How to generate unlimited leads.
- How to close.
- How to handle objections with confidence and ease.
- The fastest way to increase your sales results.
- And much more.

This conference call is free to you and everyone in your network. Tell everyone you know in sales about this free conference call.
www.ericlofholm.com/conference-call.php

Eric Lofholm International proudly offers the following products and services:

- One-on-One Sales Coaching
- Sales Consulting
- Sales Seminars
- In-House Training
- Podcast Training
- Audio Programs
- Sales DVDs
- Conference Calls
- Books

To learn how Eric Lofholm International can help you increase your sales results, call:

888.81.SALES